SIMPLY FREE

The end of your spiritual quest
for enlightenment

Oliver Bosshard

SIMPLY FREE

The end of your spiritual quest
for enlightenment

∞

SATSANG

Oliver Bosshard
2014

Copyright © 2014 by Oliver Bosshard

All rights reserved. This book or any portion thereof may not be reproduced or used in any manner whatsoever without the express written permission of the publisher except for the use of brief quotations in a book review or scholarly journal.

ISBN 978-3-033-03566-9

Oliver Bosshard
CH-8400 Winterthur
Switzerland

www.oliverbosshard.com

∞

To Mona

∞

CONTENTS

INTRODUCTION 1

WHAT THIS BOOK CONTAINS 3

DO I REALLY NEED THIS BOOK? 5

MANUAL FOR READING A NON-DUALISTIC BOOK 6

SEARCHING FOR THE END OF FEAR 8

UNAVOIDABLY THINKING YOURSELF AWAY FROM ONENESS 8

DON'T TRY TO UNDERSTAND THE HUMAN MIND 10

THE FIVE ERRORS OF THE SPIRITUAL QUEST 12

ERROR NO. 1: THERE IS A KEY TO ENLIGHTENMENT 12

ERROR NO. 2: YOU NEED TO PASS THROUGH A GATE OF ENLIGHTENMENT 13

ERROR NO. 3: YOU NEED FREE WILL TO BE FREE 14

ERROR NO. 4: YOU NEED SPIRITUAL PRACTICE 15

ERROR NO. 5: LIFE NEEDS A MEANING 18

QUESTIONS AND ANSWERS 19

I AM, ALTHOUGH I THINK 19

THOUGHT CAROUSELS AND PHILOSOPHICAL SOPHISTRIES 37

I AM … WHAT ACTUALLY AM I? 49

THE SELF IS ALSO THE SELF – FUNNY QUESTION TIME 56

I'M ALSO A QUACK DOCTOR 58

LET GO OF THE LETTING GO 59

FROM GURUS AND OTHER PROJECTION SURFACES 60

HELLO, BEING IS SPEAKING 68

GOOD TIMES, BAD TIMES 69

AM I ENLIGHTENED NOW, OR WHAT? 71

THE AUTHOR.. 74

THE ESSENCE... 75

I would like to take this opportunity to thank everybody who has supported me in writing this book. In particular I would like to thank Mona, Thomas, Caroline, Mario, Isabelle, Beat and Marco.

Thanks a lot to Helen for proofreading my English translation. You are simply the best!

∞

∞

'Everything is ONE.'

∞

INTRODUCTION

Are you looking for ways to become ONE with everything? Are you looking for happiness, eternal life and boundless freedom? For God or for the meaning of life? Do you believe that there must be something 'more'? Do you meditate, maybe with the intention of becoming enlightened, even if you don't really like to admit it? Are you part of a spiritual or religious community, but not always truly in tune with its intentions? Are you trying hard to live consciously in the here and now?

If you can reply 'yes' to some of these questions, then you are the perfect person to read this book. But be warned! A lot of things in your life could change. It might be that the person you now think you are disappears, complete with all the attendant existential and spiritual questions and longing for Oneness. Yes, dear reader, this is a risk you have to take, because your questions will only be answered with the disappearance of the person you believe yourself to be now.

Don't worry, I'm not talking about your physical body disappearing. This marvel of nature can stay alive. No, I'm talking about the disappearance of the small and very limited personal ego, the 'mini-me' as I would like to call it from now on. You know it only too well. In your head it constantly analyses and comments on your life, like a narrator transforming your thoughts into an audio book. You are tired of the noise this voice makes in your head. You want to get rid of the 'mini-me', to 'transform' it, because you think it hides your True Self.

I have good news for you! Your True Self doesn't care whether there is a 'mini-me' or not. The 'mini-me' just appears, like everything else in this apparent world of duality, out of that which you truly are, out of non-dual Oneness, out of your True Self. Like a wave in the Ocean of Being. And this Being is 'ego-less', completely impersonal.

But what exactly is this 'True Self', this mysterious 'Oneness' I am talking about? Oneness is always now, at this moment. Oneness just is. There is nothing other than Oneness. Some may call it 'Being', some 'Source', 'True Self' or 'Divine Essence'. There are infinite names for Oneness. Oneness cannot be reached by a somebody and nothing has to be changed to reveal Oneness. Oneness cannot be understood by the human mind and it cannot be accurately described with words. The words in this book can only serve as a pointer to Oneness, to a place which can never be reached, because it's always here, in every moment. The final realisation of Oneness doesn't occur BECAUSE of the words in this book, but, if you will, IN SPITE of them. The book is neither necessary for the realisation of Oneness, nor could it impede it. The law of cause and effect belongs to the world of duality. In Oneness, the world of duality has no relevance.

The last step of the spiritual journey, the 'leap into enlightenment', cannot and need not be taken, because there is no journey, nor enlightenment, nor somebody who could be doing all of this. Oneness was, is and remains Oneness. Spiritual search and enlightenment are the same.

∞

WHAT THIS BOOK CONTAINS

I'm sure you have experienced long and exciting afternoons in the spiritual section of your local bookstore, and felt the compulsion to order more and more books through the internet. Perhaps you've made the firm intention that THIS will now be the very last book about 'Satsang/Now/Non-Dualism', because you know that everything that can be said has already been said, and all this adds up to a lot of money.

I know that only too well from my 'former' life. That's why I decided to write your very last book about non-dualism. You are reading it now.

Strictly speaking, this book contains nothing. Any toddler can confirm this. It's just some nicely bound paper with a few spots of ink on it[1]. Nevertheless we are able to create a content. That's because of our conditioning, or rather, the conditioning of the 'body-mind-complex' that we generally call 'me'. Evolution and intensive training in human society allow the mind to interpret these ink spots and assign to them a deeper meaning.

The meanings formed by the spiritual mind[2] from these ink spots point to something beyond any interpretation. They point to a mystery best explained by the simple fact that what we are looking at is paper and ink spots. But most of the time this simple but true fact is not sufficient to satisfy the spiritual mind of a person wanting to reach enlightenment. A spiritual mind wants to be fed with information to think about, to analyse and classify. 'Paper and ink spots! Does this mean that I could have just picked up any piece of printed paper?', asks the spiritual mind. Yes, absolutely.

---

[1] E-book readers: Just imagine reading a 'regular' book.
[2] The part of the mind that is looking for enlightenment.

It may be that the mind, if it manages to go along with this book, suddenly surrenders and something appears that had apparently been hidden for a long time. It's THIS, the ONE which just IS: the Beingness that doesn't differentiate between paper, ink spots and words. It's what you REALLY are. Oneness. And from then on this book is no longer necessary.

∞

'My book doesn't want to make you a better person. It just wants to show you that you are already free right now.'

∞

DO I REALLY NEED THIS BOOK?

Actually, I should have had this book made from chocolate. That way it would be much easier for you to let go of it after reading, simply by gobbling it up. But for now it's a normal book made of paper and printing ink. After finishing it, you could give it to somebody as a present, or you could sell it on the internet. You might also put it on your bookshelf and encourage your friends to buy it too (that's my personal favourite, by the way!). Or you could put it on your family altar and read a few lines every morning, just as happens with many so-called 'holy books' every day, all over the world. It doesn't matter what you do with this book. You will still be the same before and after reading it: Oneness. At most your mind may have accumulated a few more words and concepts.

I use many words to describe Oneness. I am trying to describe what is literally beyond words. You may ask yourself why on earth this guy is writing a book about something which can't be described. Good question. I have no idea. There is no 'why'. It is just what is happening right NOW, at this very moment, here, with you, dear reader. It is what arises at this moment from the Ocean of Being. It is perfect. It is exactly what you are looking for. There is never more and never less.

Happy reading!

∞

MANUAL FOR READING A NON-DUALISTIC BOOK

Whether you read this book or any other text; it's basically always the same: A familiar voice in your head tells you the storyline. You believe that 'you' are this voice, because it is the same voice that comments on your life all the time. It's the voice of the 'mini-me'. At some point in time you began to identify with that voice because it was constantly present. You became used to it, just as you became used to your face in the mirror.

But have you ever asked yourself whether this voice is really 'you'? Couldn't it be just any voice, in the same way that one of 'your' thoughts could actually just be a random thought? No, I'm not talking about the 'voice of God' or the voice of a second 'Higher Self'. I'm talking about 'nobody's' voice and 'nobody's' thought.

Imagine this: A voice appears. Full stop. A thought appears. Full stop. Voice and thought simply happen, for no reason, without an owner, without any meaning. If you can begin to entertain this possibility, you will be able to read this book joyfully and without difficulty. In fact you won't be reading a book, but rather 'reading will be happening'. There is a voice reading the book to you. Enjoy it. It comes directly out of Oneness. All your questions will disappear in the light of this book. In the end, all that's left is YOU. Then you are the voice AND the book. By the way: That's what you are now as well, even before reading the book, because it is THIS that always is NOW. Oneness. There has never been anything else and there never will be anything else.

Anyway, you may be wondering – what is the purpose of this book, apart from boosting the balance of the author's bank account? Well, it has no purpose. Though perhaps by the time you reach the end of the book there won't be anybody left asking this question, or asking any question about deeper meaning at all. That's when this book can be passed on to someone else. Then it has fulfilled its purpose.

∞

'Liberation is always closer than you think.'

∞

SEARCHING FOR THE END OF FEAR

UNAVOIDABLY THINKING YOURSELF AWAY FROM ONENESS

The spiritual search is one of the strongest drivers of human existence. The thought 'I am an incomplete human being, separated from Oneness' has always preoccupied the spiritual mind of human beings. It was this one tiny thought – here I call it 'the thought of separation' – that once created gods and religions. It spawns philosophical questions about the meaning of life and fuels the engine of the spiritual mind. In the end, the spiritual quest for Oneness can always be traced back to this one thought of separation that a human being starts identifying with in the first years of life. It is the strong conviction that what we are is an individual human body with a free will, separated from other bodies, finding its own way in the world. All so-called problems in a person's life can ultimately be traced back to this one thought of separation.

The spiritual search is like playing chess on an infinite board. The problem is that this game can never be won using the tactics of the human mind. The disappearance of this singular belief in separation would be equivalent to check-mate. What remains is impersonal Oneness, from which nothing is separate.

But in Oneness the spiritual mind – whose only function is to split Oneness into two or more parts (duality) – can't split anything any more. It is no longer required. In an attempt to maintain its existence, the spiritual mind continues searching for something that it can never find. With great effort the mind searches for the imaginary 'lost Oneness' and at the same time, does all it can to avoid this Oneness, as it has a mortal fear of what it could see. The mind slowly winds its way closer and closer towards this mysterious Oneness with the help of some obscure meditation methods. It then desperately tries to get used to the resulting artificial silence, which it mistakes for Oneness. It tries to prepare itself, because it believes that Oneness is different from what is NOW at this very moment. For the spiritual mind, Oneness must be attained, even deserved.

'Good morning, I'd like some enlightenment, please.'
'That will be 50 years of meditation, if you please.'
'I beg your pardon? That's far too much!
I'd rather go to the non-dual corner shop.'

∞

DON'T TRY TO UNDERSTAND THE HUMAN MIND

Well, it's quite a strange thing, this human mind. It is, essentially, just a collection of countless thoughts. Empty thoughts. An ocean of thoughts, as it were. Whenever I use the word 'mind', you can assume that I'm referring to your thinking process. This is without any judgement of whether your thinking consists of so-called 'good' or 'bad' thoughts.

The human mind is, metaphorically speaking, the perfect knife. Its sole purpose is to slice things up. Everything must be divided and integrated into a system. Without mind, everyday life could not be mastered. The problem starts, however, when that mind – let's call it 'spiritual mind' – attempts to grasp Oneness. It fails miserably, because it always immediately divides Oneness into two or more parts (duality).

The human mind is, therefore, the wrong instrument to use for investigating Oneness. That's the reason why philosophers with their sharp minds can only ever get close to Oneness. Of course they know that, but they can't help it. They adore thinking. They have chosen the right profession.

While attempting to realise Oneness, the spiritual mind always has a vague idea of what the 'enlightened state' would be like. There are as many conceptions of Oneness as there are spiritual seekers. Again and again, I meet people who tell me that they were once 'in this Oneness' for some moments, perhaps even for some days, but that they later dropped out of it again. It took me a while to get their point. I suppose that, for some time, they were in a condition which, by chance, exactly corresponded to their personal idea of Oneness and enlightenment. For the 'mini-me', who was looking for Oneness, the goal was reached during that time and the quest was over for a short period.

But enlightenment is not a condition. Enlightenment is just another concept, an empty construct of thoughts which simply arises from what you REALLY are, from Oneness, from the Ocean of Being, for no reason. There is no enlightened person. If enlightenment appears, it appears to 'nobody'. Enlightenment is equivalent to the disappearance of the person wanting to be enlightened.

Oneness is not a condition 'somebody' (a person identified with a body) can attain and keep. Conditions can change, Oneness cannot. Nobody can 'be in Oneness'. Just as water and waves are NOT IN the ocean, they ARE the ocean. The so-called 'Realisation of Oneness' could be termed as the liberation from any kind of condition. It's like living in a condition of no-condition.

∞

THE FIVE ERRORS OF THE SPIRITUAL QUEST

At this point I would like to do away with some errors that might tempt the spiritual human mind to look for enlightenment outside of that which is NOW at this moment.

ERROR NO. 1: THERE IS A KEY TO ENLIGHTENMENT

Most people have some kind of notion of causeless happiness, deep inner peace and limitless freedom rattling around in their heads. Every human being is striving after these in some way. Our individual conditioning can make our ideas of what happiness, peace and freedom look like quite different, and we also differ greatly as to how we think these things can be achieved. Conditioning, to me, means everything in the dualistic world of manifestation that has had an effect on the psychobiological machine (human body and mind) and that has made it into what it is today: genetic inheritance, relationships (parents, siblings, close friends), society, school, climate, location, universal forces, etc. It doesn't ultimately matter what occurs to a human body in this world of duality, because it has nothing to do with the essence of True Self. Being doesn't care about conditioning at all.

In the course of the spiritual quest, the logically thinking human mind may come to the recognition that it is itself creating the barrier to limitless freedom. It begins to accept the concept that it is the search for Oneness that is preventing it from experiencing Oneness. 'This quest must be abandoned since it is useless', the human mind thinks.

For the spiritual mind, giving up the spiritual quest is equivalent to complete resignation. Meanwhile it has invented a special word for this type of search: Hope. Without the spiritual quest, believes the mind, everything would be hopeless. For the spiritual mind, to give up its quest would be to die, simply an unbearable proposition.

'Logically, the key to realise Oneness must be to allow both the seeker and the hopeful one to die', concludes the mind. The problem is that it couldn't do that, even if it wanted to. Nobody can, myself included.

But here's the good news: There is no need for a key! It doesn't matter whether the spiritual mind dies or doesn't die, because mind itself already IS precisely THIS, the ONE it is looking for. Oneness, at every moment. The ONE in the role of the seeking and hoping spiritual mind that thinks it has to die. The ONE always was there and always will be there. There is nothing else. Never. You can't keep it, hoard it, write it down, give it to somebody etc. It just IS, always, at each moment. So, nothing has to happen. No key is needed. The search and the key are one. NOW.

∞

ERROR NO. 2: YOU NEED TO PASS THROUGH A GATE OF ENLIGHTENMENT

The space on the inside of a cup is the same as the space on the outside of a cup. The seeming gate between the 'two' spaces is the cup. The cup neither creates nor negates the ONENESS of the space.

The mind often holds an erroneous idea that there is a gate somewhere that has to be reached and passed through in order to achieve freedom. This is the main reason why THAT WHICH IS in each moment is not accepted as the ONE. To one day find a gate is a completely hopeless idea, because you already found and passed through it a long time ago. It's as if you were stuck in a nightmare, wishing that soon you would return to the safety and comfort of your own bed, which in fact you have never left. After awakening from that horrible dream, there will be a deep breath of relief and perhaps also a sense of exhilaration about the simplicity of the whole ordeal.

ERROR NO. 3: YOU NEED FREE WILL TO BE FREE

Free will is an illusion! For the controlling mind this concept, which says that nobody ever has any influence on what happens, is difficult to bear. At the same time, full acceptance of this concept means boundless freedom.

In other words – every moment is as it is because it cannot be any other way. The movie of life has already been shot. What you think of as your free will is simply the inevitable acting out of the script.

Everything in the seemingly dual world of manifestation, since, let's say, the beginning of this dual universe, unfolded according to the dual rules of the game, no matter whether these are known or not. The rules of the duality game make sure that every moment is as it is and thus is perfect. Everything that has ever taken place in the seeming time of the dual world has led to you reading these lines RIGHT NOW AT THIS MOMENT!

Your response to an event, or rather the action of the 'body-mind-complex' you call 'me', will always follow exactly its conditioning, which has been evolved over billions of years. The action simply happens. After the event the mind claims it as personal. By 'happens' I mean to say that, from an absolute point of view, the action has no cause under your control. Reading this, if your controlling mind attempts to initiate an action which it calls 'my free will', this, also, is exactly what has to happen in this moment. Therefore, nobody can decide to 'awaken' and nobody can teach awakening. The movie of life simply happens, without any meaning, without any purpose. The script is already written, the film is shot and every character is played by you. You are the screen on which the film is projected, you are the light and you are the audience. You are even the popcorn. There is no conflict between the actors in the film, the light and the screen. They simply happen. Just leave them alone and allow the film of your life to run. Let it happen and do not worry about it. It happens anyway. Drink a cup of tea and feed the cat. Live your life. You are free.

∞

ERROR NO. 4: YOU NEED SPIRITUAL PRACTICE

As I mentioned before, the mind of a spiritual seeker often has some pre-conceived ideas of what a so-called 'state of enlightenment' might look like. We imagine light, tunnels, ecstasy, emptiness, silence, omniscience, egolessness, absence of will, desirelessness, thoughtlessness, etc. The searching person is always sure that the enlightened state is different from the current state. 'Different' meaning that something has to happen or something has to be done to change the current state.

Because of this misleading assumption, countless methods have been developed to induce this 'enlightened state', which is of course simply an idea constructed by the human mind. These methods are probably familiar to most of you from your own experience: meditation practices, asceticism, divine devotion, abstinence, religious practices, rituals etc. The concept behind these practices is that there is somebody, the 'mini-me', which is able to reach a certain state called enlightenment or realisation of the true self.

In the world of duality each effect needs a cause. The dual mind therefore begins to search for the cause which, for example, led to the enlightenment of Buddha. The seeker analyses the life of the enlightened person and starts to live like him, hoping that these life practices will lead him to enlightenment too. This strange idea is underpinned by reports of enlightened masters in Himalayan monasteries, tramping barefoot through the snow, levitating and nourishing themselves with light alone. Essentially the mind constructs an idealised image of an enlightened person which can never be reached. Therefore it remains busy with exercises, rituals and spiritual cleansing forever. To imagine that nothing CAN be done to bring about so-called 'enlightenment' is almost unbearable for the spiritual mind. Having to accept that the tried and tested rules of the dual world are completely useless in this special case is, for the mind, quite unimaginable and frightening. But if the mind can be open to the possibility that nothing has ever been separate from the 'enlightenment' it has been looking for, it can really have the wind taken out of its sails.

Of course nothing is bad about torturing oneself with asceticism. It's simply what appears in the dual world for that special body-mind-complex called 'ascetic'. It's perfect.

Something else that can appear, especially in spiritual/esoteric/religious settings, is the identification with a community which gives a feeling of Oneness. The collective practice of rituals and Far Eastern forms of meditation can be very enjoyable, especially within a group. But at the same time, also a kind of fear can appear. 'Maybe I won't need my beloved community anymore once I become enlightened', the mind tells itself. 'Do I really want this?' Let me tell you this: Whether you live in a spiritual community or belong to a guinea-pig breeding club is completely irrelevant in this case. Both IS the ONE and both can be great fun. Your spiritual community and your doubts about what will happen 'after the enlightenment' are ONE. There is no separation. You can neither cause, nor avoid enlightenment, because both causing and avoiding are the invitation of the ONE to see that enlightenment is ALWAYS NOW at this moment. Whether you still like to practice meditation or be a member of the local guinea-pig breeding club 'afterwards' depends on the conditioning of the body-mind-complex which you call 'me'.

Everything simply happens. Let it happen or change something; it isn't in your hands anyway. You are ONE in spite of meditation groups and guinea-pig breeding clubs. Everything appears IN you.

What I would like to tell you about the subject 'exercises for attaining enlightenment' is this: Practising something with the intention of acquiring a skill will always be connected with a certain effort in the dual world, even if this effort is very small. The thought pattern is this: You have to struggle to reach something, or at least you have to act in a certain way. The idea of the spiritual mind is always the same: There is 'somebody' (the 'mini-me') who can move from one state to another, in this case from the state of non-enlightenment to the state of enlightenment.

Let us take the subject 'meditation' as an example. The practice of meditation is designed to slow down the stream of thoughts and to condition the body-mind-complex in such a way that it becomes more serene, level-headed, mindful, conscious, etc. These character traits are highly estimated by human societies in this dual world of manifestation, because they are regarded as 'spiritual', 'holy' or 'religious'. A holy person should not stray outside of the realms of placidity as this would not fit our general idea of what a holy person should look like. The increased serenity that can result from the practice of meditation is a kind of by-product of the search for enlightenment. Essentially, the goal of meditation is the attainment of enlightenment, even if few meditators would admit it. The most famous man to represent this image was, of course, Buddha, the pop star of the enlightened, who imposed upon himself a strict meditation practice.

But simply TO BE does not require any effort, since it's the most natural thing. So the question of what meditation has to do with enlightenment can also be posed in this way: What does the baking of French baguettes have to do with it? The answer is: Nothing, respectively everything. The effort to reach enlightenment only ends with the complete abandonment of the search for enlightenment. Then the searching person disappears. Meditation methods remain or are given up. Baking French baguettes remains or is given up. In the end, there is Love. Oneness. And of course fresh French baguettes...

∞

ERROR NO. 5: LIFE NEEDS A MEANING

What is the meaning of life? This is one of the most frequent questions of the reflecting mind. 'Should THIS have been everything?' In a final summary the human mind tries to assign meaning to what has been and what it has called 'my' life. It will find one very easily. For the mind, which has spent a lifetime reflecting on whether an action makes sense or not, there should be no problem in constructing some kind of meaning at the end of life. 'To give a meaning', means that an action has led to something that I'm able to classify as 'good' within my educated value system.

Generally, every action in the dual world of the human mind is a kind of horse-trade. The mind always acts according to these rules. Everything has to make sense, and if it doesn't make sense at first sight, it will surely make sense after some investigation, at least at a 'higher level'. The idea that life is meaningless and simply happens is not easy for the spiritual mind. However, as a concept or as a pointer to the truth, this image can be extremely liberating. My concept for you is: 'There is nobody here to whom anything could be happening'. There is only impersonal 'happening'. Without any cause and any sense. It has nothing to do with YOU as Essence, what you REALLY are, Being. Let life live you! You are only the observer. The film has already been shot. From an 'absolute' point of view you can't change anything. It's all perfect.

QUESTIONS AND ANSWERS

I AM, ALTHOUGH I THINK

'Enlightened' people always talk about the 'I AM' as the key to everything. I don't understand this. I can't imagine the 'I AM' at all.

No you can't, neither can I. The 'I AM' is unimaginable. The impersonal 'I AM' is a conundrum for the human mind, which constantly ties it together with the identity of a personal 'me' (including the body). The presence of the impersonal and ever-available 'I AM' will only be accepted once this identifying thought falls away. The 'I AM' will then be experienced as a kind of keynote of ALL-ENCOMPASSING impersonal existence. This is Oneness. This feeling is in fact perfectly familiar to you, since it is always here now, the resonant keynote in the symphony of life.

Do not concern yourself with the 'I AM'. You cannot and you do not need to understand it. Relax and carry on about your business. The 'I AM' is always present, in every situation.

∞

Talking about 'Awakening' and 'Oneness': Can you tell me what exactly happened to you? Did something actually happen?

Yes and no, apparently. It seems that something did happen, otherwise this book wouldn't exist. On the other hand I write that nothing has to happen to make you what you already are. Paradoxical, right?

My search for 'the lost paradise' is a typical seeker story. It started in my earliest childhood with the beginning of the apparent separation from

Oneness. Before the appearance of the thought of separation there was only Oneness. There wasn't any separation between subject (me) and object (you). Indeed my mother's eyes were seen, but it was not yet 'mum' who was watching me. There were simply two eyes.

In the first years of my life the thought of separation appeared, together with a deep longing. A feeling of having lost something wonderful. That was the beginning of the unconscious search for 'Oneness', the search for this once known peace.

The fact, that that for which I was searching was always here and had never gone anywhere, was simply forgotten. I overlooked the closest and most obvious thing. The spiritual mind began looking for something it could never find, like an eye which tries to look upon itself. It's a hopeless struggle. But even this struggle is part of leela, the absolutely divine game known as life.

Very soon the search for Oneness led me down various religious and spiritual paths. I thought they were better suited to find THAT which in fact had never been lost. I started to accumulate concepts in my mind which I scrambled together from thousands of pages of spiritual literature. These concepts of Oneness were incredibly interesting and intellectually logical. They were gobbled up by my spiritual mind and contributed in changing the conditioning of the body-mind-complex called 'my body'. I became more calm, more aware, less aggressive. But that which I was searching for remained out of reach for the mind.

All these concepts almost drove me crazy. My head was overflowing with thoughts, until one day, the words of so-called Neo-Advaita books and transcripts of Satsangs suddenly began to resonate in my body. These words advised me to leave all these concepts behind and to stop searching. Not to care about the concepts 'enlightenment', 'liberation' and 'eternal happiness' any more. I should be quiet, go home, drink a cup of tea and read the newspaper. Wow, what an unbelievable freedom! Deep inside I knew that these words must be true and didn't question them again.

Clarity appeared one night. I fell asleep with the deep conviction that any approaching change in the current state would be a good thing, even the biggest change possible, namely death. I went to sleep with a deep trust that this kind of death wouldn't mean the death of the physical body, but rather the death of the 'mini-me', the tiny thought of separation.

Suddenly, in the space of just a moment, the opposing states of 'deep sleep', 'dreaming' and 'wakefulness' all dissolved, and with them, any sense of being a separate person, the identification with a separate 'I' thought. The event was totally unspectacular, since Being is the most familiar thing there is. There were no accompanying explosions in the brain, or tunnels of light, or supernatural visions. Aha, so it's just so incredibly simple! The border between deep sleep and waking, between life and death, between good and bad suddenly ceased to exist.

Just to make things clear; this is the very personal story of the 'body-mind-complex' named Oliver. It's one of many. A tiny wave on the Ocean of Being. But here we are not interested in the physical or mental experiences of a small, individual wave. Everything can emerge from Being. But that which appears can also disappear. Sooner or later. Maybe. It cannot be held on to. The Truth held on to is no longer Truth. The realisation of this fact means total liberation, but for nobody, since there is no longer anybody there who could personalise it.

The only thing which is always here is a keynote of existence. This keynote is, in a way, the smallest possible expression of Oneness in the human body. Everything else is a concept of the mind, this collection of thoughts, which does nothing other than ceaselessly creating concepts. The keynote, the 'I AM', always effortlessly present, is the very basis of the world, which appears in me. Without this 'I AM', there is no world. It's the first thought that arises out of consciousness and creates an apparently dual world. A world which is, in fact, only a thought form.

This basic feeling had always been present. It was with me all the time. It's the closest thing there is. It's the only thing that REALLY is. It's Oneness. The 'I AM', 'I EXIST' is so close that you constantly overlook it. It's like a pair of glasses that you have been looking through all the while but had forgotten that you were wearing them. It's the most evident thing there is. It makes itself known in the absence of the mind that wants to keep and understand it. As soon as the mind is quiet for a brief moment, it's here. When mind ceases to classify and analyse it, it's here. Then the mind leaves it in peace and attends to its daily business, in its function as a working and organising mind. The body-mind-complex, formerly identified as a person named Oliver, continues to operate perfectly well in accordance with its conditioning through heritage, socialization and life experience. But there is no longer anybody there to become involved in the leela, the divine game. It is recognised for what it is – a thought form ascending and descending out of the Ocean of Being like a wave. It is the dance of life.

∞

You say that the body-mind-complex doesn't change after the awakening. But what about emotions? Are they different now?

Your question implies the assumption that enlightenment is a state which is different from the state of non-enlightenment. In fact enlightenment isn't a state which can be reached and possessed by a person. If you like, enlightenment can be described as the state of the stateless. This means that things may change and they may not. The same can be said for emotions (feelings like joy, grief, anger, etc.), which are nothing other than energies stored in the body. After liberation there is no longer a person, no authority figure, wanting to change or control things. Changes simply happen. Emotions simply happen, just as they did before. Emotions come and go, just as they always have done. Depending on the conditioning of the person (temperament, character, etc.), emotions differ from human being to human being.

Metaphorically speaking, emotions can be compared with waves on the ocean of life. They come and go, sometimes stronger, sometimes weaker. You are the ocean and the waves are the ocean too, no matter how high they are.

∞

Exactly these waves are very high in my case. I have fantasies in my head, which are a distraction; they throw me out of balance and weaken me. My mind goes round and round in circles. It really bothers me.

Consider that everything, every fantasy and every resistance to this fantasy is just another thought. And, basically, thoughts are NOTHING. They are empty. They come and go like waves on the ocean and clouds in the sky. Whether these thoughts are so-called fantasies or projections, or whether it's the ONE thought of identification with a separate person; who cares? Why should I give my utmost attention to these few tiny little scraps of the billions of thoughts which are constantly arising and subsiding? It sometimes seems to me to be almost an addiction to these few little thoughts which are described as 'bad' or 'annoying' according to a human mind's value scale.

Being (ocean) doesn't care whether there are thoughts (waves) or not. Thoughts in the form of the working mind are present all the time and are mostly very useful in daily life. Complete silence, which is sought for example during meditation, doesn't result from the cessation of thoughts but from the cessation of the person who identifies itself with these thoughts. The thoughts are not the problem.

So don't worry about your fantasies. They are only thoughts. They come and they go, without rhyme or reason. What remains all the time is YOU. It was and always will be YOU. Oneness.

∞

I have a 'turbulent consciousness'. What do you recommend to me?

I suppose you mean by a 'turbulent consciousness' that you think and dream a lot. Perhaps you have strong so-called 'negative' emotions like anger, inferiority complexes, fear, feelings of guilt, etc. Let me tell you this:

Since you ask what to do, it seems you want to get rid of the 'turbulent consciousness', right? It bothers you being like that. You would like to be different. Perhaps you think that in some way a 'calm consciousness' or a 'calm character' is better. Maybe you believe you will be happier if you dream and think less, or if you are emotionally calm and controlled.

In this case you automatically associate happiness with certain conditions which have to occur first in order for you to be happy. But I can tell you that unimaginable happiness and endless freedom are here now in this moment! They are not hidden and not clouded, nor are they somewhere deep 'inside you'. They are EXACTLY THIS, THAT WHICH IS RIGHT NOW. Nothing will ever be different.

A dualistically-minded spiritual teacher would perhaps say: 'You should meditate to calm your thoughts. You should affirm and create your world as you wish to see it. You should think positively, send out love, firmly believe in the goodness of life and see that you are the creator of the universe.' That's fine. Maybe your conditioning will heed this advice, maybe not. If it seems easy enough and it sounds like fun, you will probably try it out. These are all magical games in the dual world which can make things easier for the psycho-biological machine, or so-called 'human being'. You can join the game or not. Whether you join or not isn't in your hand. Nobody has an influence on it because the film of life is already shot. Anyway, what YOU ARE never changes. What you REALLY ARE, Being, not separate from the 'turbulent consciousness' nor from the thought 'I have to do something to get rid of my turbulent consciousness', is ALWAYS present.

To experience unbelievable bliss and endless peace right now means to accept that nothing has to be done. The gift – which can also be called Grace – is always here. Grace is always present. Grace is the only thing there is. Grace can't be given to somebody and you can't prepare for it. Grace is the invitation from Being to itself to accept that everything, in this and in every moment, is already whole and complete. Being doesn't know any Grace because it is Grace itself.

You could say that finding happiness involves making peace with the person (the 'mini-me') who is looking for happiness and who thinks they have to do something in order to achieve it. The person is this way because they are the way they are. They cannot be otherwise. The person IS the happiness that is searched for. The search will dissolve with the acceptance of this fact. Afterwards there won't be anybody left who feels bothered by the 'turbulent consciousness'. It is revealed as unimaginable happiness and endless peace, that which it had already always been.

∞

But does the 'mini-me', let's say during a personal life crisis, have enough power to dissolve willingly in Oneness? Isn't resistance and fight useless if the film of life has already been shot?

The 'mini-me' can use as much power as it likes; it cannot dissolve itself. The disappearance of the tiny thought 'I am a separate person', which is in fact the basis of the existence of the 'mini-me', requires so LITTLE power that the mind can't even begin to imagine. If anything, a personal crisis might actually help the process of 'letting go'. Some dualistic teachers may suggest that a personal life crisis could serve as a kind of 'gate to enlightenment'. Unfortunately this statement can be misunderstood by the 'mini-me', which starts to think that it needs to do something in order to make 'IT' happen, for example to suffer or to go through a crisis, which is, of course, totally unnecessary.

'The film is already shot' means that in the apparent world of duality the 'body-mind-complex' and the thought-formed 'mini-me' will behave in the way they must behave; in the way that has been conditioned since the beginning of the dual world. That's why every moment is perfect, because it cannot be otherwise. Every apparent action – with each one just a single moment in the timeless NOW – is always a predetermined reaction to previous events. Whether resistance and struggles appear in the film or not is all interrelated.

All this happens IN the Being, in the Oneness, in the real I, in that which you truly are. But only apparently, because it's still a concept of mind and in fact nothing needs to happen. You don't have to be woken up because you are not sleeping.

∞

Please help our minds again: Are we the actors in the film of life, or the film itself, or the screen or only the spectators?

You are all actors in the film and you are the audience in the cinema. You are the screen, the film, the projector and the light. You are also the seat. And you are the popcorn and M&Ms. No part of this cinematographic event is separate from the others. Just enjoy this experience of life, because that's why it's here!

∞

I have to come back to the body-mind-complex again: How do you deal with sadness or anger? How with problems in general?

Emotions like anger or sadness just appear as part of the conditioning of the 'psycho-biological machine', the so-called human being. Anger remains as anger. Acts occur to reduce or transform the anger. Sadness remains as sadness, pain remains as pain. There is just sadness. There is just pain. The ocean is still the ocean, even with very huge waves.

Please allow me a short dualistic remark: There are of course some methods of 'brainwashing' that can be utilised in order to change the conditioning of human beings in order to solve problems in their daily life. Some of these methods are very effective and can help to facilitate communication and the cooperation of people in this world of manifestation. I am thinking of the method of 'Nonviolent Communication' by Marshall Rosenberg, which I can warmly recommend, or of the epic work 'A Course in Miracles' by Helen Schucman. Other methods like, for example, practices of meditation are used to control body and mind. Of course these methods have no influence on the Being because they ARE the Being. They are in a way another characteristic in the game of life.

By the way: 'Non-violence' has nothing to do at all with having no will. 'To turn the other cheek', which is THE Christian metaphor for non-violence, means that everything that happens is welcomed and that nothing is judged by anyone, even if it is a returning slap in the face. Whatever happens, and no matter what kind of actions appears: All is perfect. It is happening in perfect undiscriminating Love and Oneness.

∞

What exactly is total acceptance? What happens in the mind/body? Somehow the mind always interferes when a situation, or past occurrences, or illness have to be accepted. I believe that is its nature. As soon as I get involved in something, my mind starts to rattle. When does one accept something completely?

My key word for you concerning perfect acceptance is 'inclusiveness'. 'Total inclusiveness', without exceptions. If you apply this concept to 'acceptance' by including everything that appears, you will see that total acceptance has nothing to do with the acceptance of a situation. Even if your mind cannot accept a situation, it can accept that it cannot accept a situation. The mind can also accept that it cannot accept that it cannot accept a situation. You can weave this on and on, but there is always somebody who thinks he has to accept something. Therefore, your mind will never be able to accept something totally. Total acceptance and complete inclusiveness result in the disappearance of the person thinking they have to accept something.

Regarding the mind: When the mind is busy with something, it naturally starts 'rattling' (starts working), because that is its purpose and that purpose is very helpful in daily life. With a correctly used mind you can create everything. But you can't liberate yourself with your mind, because you cannot think yourself away. Therefore I always say that you can stop torturing your mind with these kind of questions. Relax, because you are free right NOW (hmm, funny, didn't I say that already?).

∞

Speaking of action: How can I know that I act with the right motives? What is a right motive for an action?

In general there are no right or wrong motives for an action. Decisions are made and there is no need for an 'owner' of these decisions, because there is no one who has an influence on what decision is made. It may sound strange for the mind but there is no such thing as free will. FREE WILL IS AN ILLUSION. The acceptance of this fact means total liberation.

I know that the judging mind often has some difficulty in making decisions. But, as I said before, the film of life is already shot. The 'right' decision is already made, whether the mind has difficulty deciding or not. The decision, however it may be, is always perfect. It has to be. Judgements like 'right' or 'wrong', 'good' or 'bad' dissolve in Oneness.

Of course you can change your mind after your first decision. Your mind may find a logical sequence of arguments giving you a reason to make a new decision. Afterwards, the mind will say there was a wrong motive behind the first decision. It can decide again and again millions of times. These are still actions which simply happen. When the time has come for an action, it happens, no matter what the motives.

∞

Wait a minute. You say that everything is without reason, without meaning. There is nothing to do and nothing to meditate on etc. In that case could you please explain to me why you, Karl Renz, Eckhart Tolle, Samarpan, Tony Parsons, etc. give Satsangs, write books and coach people? And why then should we send our children to school?

You can't do anything that could turn you into something that you already ARE. It's like the metaphor of the glasses which are already on your nose. Regarding Oneness, it doesn't matter if you meditate, write books, give Satsangs, teach children, send them to school, help poor people, make war, pray, watch a soccer match, etc. It is what appears for the body-mind-complex you call 'me'. In other words, they are manifestations which happen IN what you REALLY are. People who ask questions and think that they have free will ALWAYS act in a perfect way, even if they believe that they don't. Perhaps they start to write books because they have a talent for it and enjoy writing. Or they think that they HAVE to write books because it is expected of them. Or because they feel an urgent need to write. There are billions of influences which make a person act in a certain way. The person has no influence on what kind of actions will appear. The film is already shot.

I understand that initially this concept is quite scary for a person who is convinced that they have free will. This person might say: 'But I can make new decisions at every moment. I can change myself and become a better person.' Maybe you can, maybe not. That's written in the script of life too. It's the perfect script.

Surprisingly, this concept can be unbelievably liberating for a person. The fear of death that the 'mini-me' has quickly decreases, and an acceptance that nothing can be done appears. Eventually, the 'mini-me' disappears and suddenly there is just happiness without cause. The ONE. And there is no longer the need for spiritual concepts like 'free will'.

∞

But if our life is pre-determined, does this mean that we can't do anything? That everything happens as it should happen? Everything is 'God's Plan' so to speak?

Life, the world, the universe simply happen. EVERYTHING simply happens, without any plan and cause, without time and space. The human mind, believing itself to be a separate person with its own will, simply happens. Decisions and actions happen without them being anybody's decisions or actions. After every 'happening' you can add an 'apparently', since in fact, nothing actually 'happens' at all. There is only Oneness. You are endlessly free. You are the feather in the wind. And you are the wind.

∞

When I hear you tell me that I don't have free will and that I can't do anything in order to feel better, I feel very stressed. I'm impatient and want to do something to change the situation. I can't just hang around and wait.

It's totally normal that you feel stressed by the thought that you don't have a free will. But this 'you' is just a tiny little thought which has constructed a huge edifice named 'I am a separate individual' and which is now trying to defend the edifice by all means possible. If you try to maintain the concept of free will, then at the same time you keep alive the state of the 'mini-me'. And that's a very exhausting undertaking, isn't it?

When I talk to you I never talk to you as an apparent individual. I'm not interested at all in the individual even if in the beginning this might sound heartless to you. I'm talking to you as Oneness, as if I were talking to myself. You, what you really are, Oneness, pure alive existence, don't have to do anything at all in order just to BE. This 'JUST BEING' is always endless freedom and happiness, even if the apparent 'me' is unhappy, doesn't feel free or is even depressed.

You ask what you can do because you are impatient. Well, what do you normally do? What do you like to do? What do you do voluntarily, without being pushed into it by somebody? It can be anything, for example reading, eating, watching television, playing soccer, meditating, boxing, sleeping, working, sitting on a chair, reading the newspapers, drinking coffee, etc. It doesn't matter what it is.

I would suggest that, if you want to do something, just do those things which don't require an effort for you, things that you enjoy doing. Forget about my concept of not having a free will, the concept of the endless happiness and freedom that you've been searching for and just let life live you. That's all! You can't escape.

To believe that everything is ONE frightens me more than it makes me happy, because I feel completely alone. I feel so lonely with this image.

That's because the mind automatically puts 'being alone' on the same level with 'being lonely'. To be completely alone doesn't mean to be lonely. Only a separate ME who can't imagine being without other separate ME's could have the idea that a world without other ME's would be lonely.

In complete Oneness, emptiness isn't felt as loneliness but as fusion with EVERYTHING. It could be equated with the words 'freedom', 'peace' and 'happiness'. Since Oneness isn't personal, it doesn't require any 'others' to grant it freedom, peace or happiness. The 'others' are Oneness too.

∞

In Satsang and Advaita talks I often hear the following answers to the question of a seeker: 'To whom does this appear?' Or: 'Is there nobody who understands this?' I don't understand what this means. Is it related to the 'mini-me' or to consciousness, to Being?

Basically in Satsang there is always this one counter question: 'WHO asks the questions?' The investigation of this counter question by the identified mind (the apparent person who asks questions in Satsang) leads to a kind of loop. The answer can never be found by the person enquiring; with the 'understanding' of the answer, the identification of a person ceases to exist. In the end there isn't anybody left to 'keep' or 'conserve' the answer. There is nobody who could have the final realisation of Oneness because realisation is the recognition that there is only THIS, the One. There is no 'either... or' in Oneness, and therefore no questions and no answers remain.

This doesn't mean that the seekers should ask themselves who is this 'me' who is asking the questions. It is unnecessary. There is only Oneness. The 'me' who is asking questions is Oneness appearing as an apparent 'me' who is asking questions. So nothing has to be done. Liberation is NOW. You may relax and let 'it' happen, because it has already happened.

∞

I'd like to return to the Truth: 'With the understanding of the answer, identification ceases'. How can the 'mini-me' quickly disappear in order that the answer appears? How can the 'mini-me' trust and let go? Is it the fear of dying which hinders it? Does the 'mini-me' have to die voluntarily? Please give us a metaphor.

Relax! Take it easy! You can neither do anything nor do you have to. You don't have to let go of anything, you don't have to die, you don't even have to be relaxed (again this sounds like a paradox). Nothing needs to be changed because the answer is already here. It is only the search for the answer which prevents you from recognising it.

Here is a dualistic bedtime treat for you (caution, dear hardcore-nondualists, please don't give up on me! Just close your eyes and ears for a moment):

If you like you can try to get a feeling into your body which unconsciously you know very well. It's a memory from the time when you were lying in the cradle as a baby. It's a kind of unconditional trust that everything is perfect, including the conditioned actions and habits of 'your' body-mind-complex, even if you consider them not to be very spiritual or 'good' (hunger, stomach ache, defecating, etc.). Acquaint yourself with the concept that a free will – in absolute terms – is an illusion. What you think you are, the 'mini-me', is a feather in the wind, a wave on the ocean, a lily of the field (you see, others have tried to explain that too before).

Good luck!

∞

Sometimes I feel sad. Can you tell me what true consolation is?

True consolation (or true healing) is only possible in the timeless presence of Being. Where separation and therefore suffering no longer exist, the suffering person who needs consolation and the person who wants to soften the suffering by giving consolation are both recognised as one. Then separation between the suffering and the consoling person no longer exists. Suffering and consolation are recognised – by no one – as the ONE appearing as two.

∞

To whom does the idea of death refer?

The idea of death refers to the separate person, who believes that they were born and hence that they will die. Seen from the perspective of True Self, nothing is ever born and nothing is going to die. Birth and death are illusions, concepts of mind constructed by an apparent separate person who is identified with a body. When the person disappears, the idea of birth and death will disappear too. Birth, death and reincarnation, whether in heaven, on earth, or in hell are all recognised as the ONE playing the game of life.

∞

THOUGHT CAROUSELS AND PHILOSOPHICAL SOPHISTRIES

You say that everything is one. So a tree is just the ONE appearing as a tree, right? But how is it possible for the unmanifest, attribute-less and boundless ONE to appear as a tree (maya) in consciousness?

To say that a tree is an expression of the ONE is of course merely a concept for the human mind that wants to have some kind of image of what's going on. It's a kind of mental practice, like maya (the illusory world) or leela (the divine game), which are also just concepts. In reality there is no tree. Nothing ever happens. The human mind is not capable of imagining Oneness because mind itself IS Oneness. Like an eye which can't see itself. In the end, every concept must be abandoned because it never leads to the Truth. Liberation means liberation from mental concepts of liberation.

The purpose of every spiritual practice (including meditation) is, if you like, to demoralise the person who wants to be liberated, to the point where he throws in the towel and stops practising. Unfortunately nobody can make this happen. But it is also completely unnecessary, since the apparent person who should stop practising is the ONE too! Nothing has to happen at all.

For this reason I keep repeating my mantra: Relax and simply do what you are already doing. EVERYTHING now and in every moment is the ONE you are looking for. Everything you can experience through your senses can be made into your altar, your guru[3]. Everything is an invitation from the One for you to accept that nothing can nor must be done.

---

[3] A guru does not necessarily need to be a person. The only thing that counts is the guru's ability to be a messenger of light in the darkness. In the example of the ferryman Vasudeva in Herman Hesse's book Siddhartha the river took on the role of guru.

Can you please explain the term 'phenomenon'? In the end a tree is nothing other than consciousness appearing to us as a tree, right?

My conditioning leads me to have a preference for using simple words to explain the ONE, because actually it's endlessly simple and anyhow there are no suitable words for it. Therefore I prefer not to introduce new terms, but I would like to return to the METAPHOR OF THE OCEAN and make it a little more palatable for you:

Imagine there is only the ocean (the ONE, Being, Consciousness, Awareness, the True Self, God). Its nature (the divine game of separation) is to create waves (manifestation, phenomena). Now imagine that our ocean consists of billions of thoughts. Its waves, which are never separated from the ocean, are just thoughts too. Empty thoughts. Nothing. So you can imagine that a tree and all phenomena are thought forms which appear in the ocean of Being and disappear again. The ocean is not concerned about the waves, even if one among billions of waves (the identified person, the thought of separation, the 'mini-me') suddenly starts to think that it is separated from the ocean. The ocean and likewise the identified person are just as they have always been, simply the ONE.

∞

Who is actually identifying with a person? Consciousness or mind?

What exactly is the difference? We may, if you like, use my favourite image of the ocean again. Imagine the mind being an accumulation of billions of thoughts arising out of the Ocean of Being like waves. Instead of 'arise' you can also say 'happen'. Thoughts just happen, mind just happens. One of these thoughts is the thought of separation, which creates an identified person (the 'mini-me'), even though, of course, there can't be any thought which is separated from Being. So there is, in a way, 'nobody' identifying with a person. You can say: Identification is appearing... and disappearing. Or not. Who cares?

Let me say this again: These are only concepts for the asking mind whose nature is to ask questions because otherwise it gets bored. In reality nothing arises and nothing happens. Linear imaginations of time and space completely disappear in Eternal Being.

∞

Is emptiness the real essence of form?

If mind can't classify the term 'emptiness' (or 'silence') then we are on the right path. Every word which mind can't classify is appropriate to describe the 'real character of form'. This way, the mind no longer concerns itself with the 'real character of form' and the questions disappear.

I would like to summarise the 'essential character of form' as follows: Form arises from the ONE, form vanishes into the ONE, form IS the ONE. Form is emptiness.

∞

Is love the link between form (fullness) and emptiness?

Love is the deep impersonal knowing that there is no need for a link between form (fullness) and emptiness.

What is an appearance in consciousness?

Imagine there are just appearances, but no one to whom they appear. They don't belong to anybody. They are not 'my' or 'your' appearances. They simply happen, without any reason, without meaning and without a creator. Just like that. It can be thoughts, objects, human beings, energy beings or whatever. Consider that these are not appearances IN consciousness, but rather consciousness itself is the appearance. It plays the game 'appearing and disappearing' with the person doing the asking. And the person itself is part of the appearance too, appearing and disappearing out of you, the Being. Timeless and spaceless.

∞

What is the difference between 'awakening' and 'liberation'? I have noticed that even strict non-dualistic teachers use these two terms.

Well, this is actually something for the division 'enlightenment for advanced practitioners'. Sometimes Satsang teachers use these two terms as a kind of guideline for recently 'awakened' persons to handle the chaos in the body-mind-complex (waves in the ocean).

One could say that awakening occurs in one single moment, and that this moment can be easily pinpointed. It is the sudden impersonal realisation that there are two ME's: The personal 'mini-me' (identification) and the impersonal ME (Oneness). It is a majestic state of wisdom where there are no more questions and where the body isn't necessary any more. But as long as the 'mini-me', which has had a front row seat for this 'awakening', wants to stay in this awakened state and hold onto it, it is trapped in something you could call a 'prison of wisdom'.

True liberation means liberation from any kind of state. Liberation occurs when the person who wants to stay in the state of being awake, disappears. This process can take some time. Nisargadatta Maharaj, for example, travelled towards the Himalaya after his initial awakening. On the way he became completely liberated and returned to his family and to his store. Metaphorically speaking, the awakened person must break out of the 'prison of wisdom' (male principle) and dissolve into the 'ocean of love' (female principle). He jumps into the dual world and loses himself in it, like the angel in the Hollywood film 'City of Angels'. After this process, when the two poles become one, there isn't an awakened person any more but simply impersonal freedom. Then everything is as it was before, hence the saying in Zen Buddhism: 'Before enlightenment chop wood carry water, after enlightenment chop wood carry water.'

∞

In your opinion, when did the identification with a personal 'me' die with Ramana Maharshi? Immediately after his near-death-experience or in the years of retreat and immersion?

In the moment of the 'death simulation', Ramana Maharshi awakened from the dream of separation. The identification with a personal 'mini-me' was seen for what it is. What followed was the path of the conditioned 'body-mind-entity' which was drawn to its favourite place, the holy mountain Arunachala in South India. Ramana's conditioning made him choose retreat and immersion, risking the death of the body, which, as we know, was prevented by some local residents. Later Ramana Maharshi again found his way into a kind of normality.

∞

Is enlightenment when consciousness becomes aware of itself?

A dualistic teaching teacher would probably define it that way. Non-dualistically seen, this definition doesn't make any sense. That's why I say that enlightenment happens when there isn't anybody left (no person) who could experience enlightenment or who could identify with the 'state of enlightenment'. That is, by the way, the reason why no master would ever confirm a student to be enlightened. Enlightenment doesn't need any confirmation, because there isn't anybody left who would ask him or herself if they are enlightened or not.

∞

Is there really nobody left? Isn't it so that, after the disappearance of the 'mini-me', the 'I AM' remains, pure presence, the space in which human being and world appear?

The 'I AM' or 'Presence' or 'Oneness' is completely impersonal. 'Nobody is here anymore' means that no person, in the literal sense of the word person, is left. Nobody is there to identify with Presence or Oneness. I can't say: 'I am pure Presence' (or Oneness, light, emptiness, fullness or whatever you would like to call it). But I can say, if you like, 'there is just pure Presence'.

∞

How would you accurately describe the state of the 'sudden awareness of just Being' in your own words? The term 'enlightenment' can be very misleading for a newcomer to seeking. So can the term 'awakening'.

I can assure you that even for an 'advanced seeker' the term 'enlightenment' can be pretty misleading. So in order to prevent an enthusiastic new seeker from becoming a frustrated advanced seeker, please take the following words to heart:

There is no state. Forget about that word. NOTHING has to change because everything is complete right NOW. So stop seeking immediately and go home or to the cinema. What you are looking for is here NOW and it cannot be found, because seeker and sought are one and the same.

I would call what you are looking for a kind of 'existence'. Being alive. It's a kind of impersonal keynote of existence, which contains EVERYTHING. The joke is that this keynote of existence is NOW with you. Always. You simply don't want to believe it, and your mind tries to find and to explain it. That's completely UNNECESSARY! You don't have to do anything.

Here another dualistic bedtime treat (sorry, again nothing for hardcore non-dualists):

If you believe that you really need to do something, just carry a feeling with you, of how it would be, if you had already found what you are looking for.

∞

You say: All is ONE. But the 'I' can't be an object, right?

When I say, in accordance with my concept, that ALL IS ONE, the 'I' is of course ONE too. In this context it doesn't matter whether you imagine your 'I' as an object or whatever else. Your idea of an 'I' is ONE too.

Can you please address the following question in your own words: 'Is there life after death? Does true life come only after death?'

'Who' asks this question? It is the one thought: 'I am a body that is separated from other bodies in a world of linear time and space.' Metaphorically speaking it is the wave that feels separated from other waves and from the ocean. When this single thought disappears and, together with it, the feeling of separation, the perception of space, time, life and death disappear too.

In Oneness the circle of life and death simply appears, just as everything simply appears and disappears. The ideas of 'life', 'death', 'life after death', 'reincarnation' and whatever else are ultimately only concepts of the separate 'mini-me'. It wants to reach a place of no suffering: Heaven, paradise, nirvana or eternity. But it won't ever experience the fact that this heaven is already here NOW, even if it reincarnates millions of times. Heaven cannot be experienced by 'somebody'. Heaven simply IS. Always NOW.

∞

Which of the two of us is God?

According to the concept that all is ONE (Being, the Ocean, Oneness, God) we are both ONE and therefore ONE with God. Just as waves are ONE with the ocean, even if one small wave believes itself to be separated from the other waves and from the ocean. Everything that happens in this world of duality is an illusion that the 'mini-me' is trapped in. It apparently happens IN God, the timeless and spaceless non-dual Oneness.

Well then, this was a spiritual-philosophical concept for your mind. You can believe it or not; it doesn't matter, because it is not a question of belief or non-belief. The wave can believe whatever it wants: It is free either way and ONE with the ocean.

You want to be free? Then don't look at the irrelevant finger of the master when he shows you the moon. Forget the attempts to link the finger (dualism) to the moon (non-dualism) with the help of mental concepts. It is neither possible nor necessary. Just have faith and look at the moon. Clarity will follow automatically.

∞

Where in this entire system does the soul range? What is it? Does it arise out of Being and communicate through the 'I'? How does it transmit itself, if the messenger 'I' is no longer there?

As you may have noticed I never use the term 'soul'. It is used very inconsistently and is interpreted in many different ways according to religion or spiritual tradition. In our Western culture the soul is known as a kind of 'ethereal personality' that outlasts the body and is re-born or not, depending on the spiritual belief. It implies a person, a character, and represents in a sense the desire of the 'mini-me' for immortality. If you like you can imagine the soul simply as a thought-form.

In my metaphor of the Ocean of Oneness, the soul – along with all (thought-) forms of the apparent world of duality – simply appears and disappears like a wave. It is, like everything else, never separated from the Ocean. It appears IN you, the Ocean, like the thought-made concepts of life, death and rebirth. If there is just Oneness and no carrier 'I', thus no separate person anymore, the concept of an ethereal individual disappears. The wave can finally remain a wave, without a 'somebody' who fusses about it. What remains is THAT which had always been. Oneness.

∞

Do you also experience your true identity in deep sleep, when your consciousness is no longer relating to objects?

There is nobody who experiences his true identity, neither in deep sleep nor in the waking state. There is no 'experiencer' of a true identity, because every experiencer IS that identity (subject = object). Just as the personal identity disappears in deep sleep (in deep sleep you don't exist), it is now absent in the waking state too. During the night 'nobody' (no person) is sleeping, and in the morning 'nobody' wakes up any more.

∞

But isn't exactly THAT proof that you must exist as a 'nobody'? Otherwise you couldn't answer because talking, writing, reading and waking in the morning are functions of consciousness too, aren't they? What else could they be?

You are trying to mix up two dimensions; the dual realm of this apparent universe and the non-dual realm, which I'm pointing to. It is not necessary to first understand 'different levels' of the dual realm before you can 'rise' to the non-dual one. It is totally irrelevant whether there are any hairs between the fingers of the master's hand pointing to the moon. That has nothing to do with the moon.

Of course you are free to imagine that there is Oneness appearing as a 'nobody'. You can replace 'nobody' by any random word that will help you to drop the idea of object and subject, of cause and effect in the dual world of illusion. Your mind clings to this 'nobody' because it cannot accept the fact that, according to my concept, forms simply emerge out of Oneness and are Oneness themselves. Without reason. Without purpose. Without cause. The mind cannot debate Oneness; it cannot prove it, because it can only divide things, which leads away from Oneness into twoness (duality). It is like the singularity before the Big Bang. It can make the mind go crazy in the attempt to understand it.

But actually it isn't necessary at all for the mind to understand this in order that liberation may occur. The so-called 'understanding' that you are looking for will automatically arise when the mind gives up. At the same time you, the identified person (the thought of separation), which is in fact responsible for all your questions, will disappear too. What remains can be called 'Nobody', 'Oneness', 'Silence', 'Being', 'True Self' or 'All', depending on the concept. There is no term for it that would be accepted by the analytical mind. The mind always wants to relate one term to other terms, which keeps it trapped in duality.

Just find out WHO it is that is asking these questions (yes, since the days of Ramana Maharshi this is THE famous Satsang question), or, even better, allow the one who asks these questions to disappear.

Comment of a reader:

'You don't have to understand the teacher. With the help of his teaching you have to free your WANTING to understand from your personal WANTING. Only then total understanding will come to you, naked and dumb. Then EVERYTHING will be seen. You will not be needed any more. I would never have thought such freedom to be possible, but Oliver's Satsang removes everything from your path. You have no choice but to be free.'

∞

I AM ... WHAT ACTUALLY AM I?

How do you go about, I mean, without a body?

As you can see there is a body. But it doesn't belong to anybody. It just happens. It appears, just as everything in the world of manifestation simply appears. 'I' do nothing. You could say that actions simply happen. Actually that was always the case. Actions simply happen in your case too. The 'mini-me' of a seeker is unfortunately always a little arrogant concerning the supposed control of actions. Like a child sitting behind the wheel of a carousel car and thinking it has total control over the vehicle.

∞

When you look at yourself in a mirror, what do you see?

Each morning the same well-known face appears in the mirror. But it doesn't belong to anybody any more. There is no longer a difference between the face in the mirror and the mirror itself.

In the manifestation, in this apparent world that emerges out of you (Being), things can change or not. It doesn't matter what seems to change. Just as the ocean doesn't care about the forms of its waves. Water remains water, Oneness remains Oneness.

∞

Who wakes up in the morning? Where are you during deep sleep?

My definition of deep sleep is that in deep sleep no person exists. There is no one to think about themself or maintain identification with a person. In other words: You cannot be somewhere in deep sleep because you don't exist there. When you wake up in the morning, the person (the 'mini-me' you think you are) wakes up together 'with you'. After the disappearance of the 'mini-me' one could say that there is just impersonal waking. In other words 'no one' wakes up in the morning. The border between deep sleep and the waking state has dissolved.

∞

You say: 'The seeking person disappears. What remains is Oneness. It is THAT which you really are and always have been.' Does this mean that I am not a human being?

The 'divine game', the illusion of being a human being is arising out of Being. What you really are, the ONE, is the keynote of the eternal symphony of life. The human being and hence also the expression of the body-mind-complex known as 'Oliver' is one of many melodies. Sometimes harmonious, sometimes dissonant, but always inseparable from the keynote.

∞

Do you believe that you are just this body-mind-organism belonging to the species of human being or are you defining yourself by the pure formless and nameless awareness?

There is no longer anybody that needs to define anything. There is just a kind of incomprehensible, impersonal knowing. Questionless clarity. Awareness. Being. Everything which appears is THIS, whether it's Oliver's body or a glass of beer. It is the ONE. Like the flower in Buddha's hand which, as he silently showed it to his disciples, was instantly recognised by one of them as the ONE. The flower is just a metaphor. Buddha could also have shown them an old shoe.

∞

Do you also recognise yourself in the waves (person) which appear IN the ocean?

Let me explain it this way: The waves remain as they always were. They are observed but not by the ocean and not by a person (wave). They are observed by 'no one'. You could say there is a kind of absolute perception, a perception which requires neither subject nor object. I know this sounds paradoxical for the human mind.

Look, the dual world (i.e. the waves, which include human bodies and thoughts of separation), arising according to my concept out of the ONE, is complete in each and every moment. It cannot help but be complete. There is nobody here to have an influence on what happens when and to whom. This dual world simply happens. Whether a wave defines itself as a person or not is completely irrelevant. There is no person with free will. Only the thought of separation thinks that there is. It personalises the wave and apparently separates itself from the other waves.

The ocean doesn't identify itself with the waves. It leaves them alone and simply IS. Even better; it doesn't even know anything of the waves. You don't worry about the exact location of each hair on your body, do you? They are, of course, inseparably part of you.

You could picture it like this: Your body happens, even if one of your tens of thousands of hairs begins to feel separate from you. You don't care at all because you don't know about it. You are the body and of course each hair belongs to you. (Except, of course, the hairs that have fallen out. Those would be the ones who have lost their religion. And with a bald head you are enlightened. Ok, let's leave it at that.)

∞

Do you not suffer anymore? Do you not get annoyed? Do you still get angry?

Of course there can be anger. Sadness or fear too, according to the conditioning of the psycho-biological machine called the human body. Everything can appear. But there is just anger, and acts may occur to calm down this anger, which is felt as a kind of energy in the body. But there aren't thoughts anymore which personify the anger, give a personal history to it, add fuel to and inflate it. Without a story, anger usually disappears very quickly. But no matter how strong anger or sadness might be – the impersonal keynote of deep peace is always present.

∞

You say that fear can also arise, even if a fearful 'mini-me' no longer exists. But how do you handle the unpleasant physical reactions?

You just said it. If there is no 'someone' left, no one is handling any physical reactions any more. They are just here. They emerge and usually disappear again quickly, because they no longer receive any energy from 'somebody' (the 'mini-me') who intensifies the reactions by identifying with them and granting them time and their own story.

∞

What is the most stunning aspect of the newfound freedom? Do you suddenly tolerate a person you never liked? Or can you enjoy a cigarette although you needed years to stop smoking?

No, you finally smack the person you never liked in the face. Joking apart, essentially nothing changes because the Being, this keynote of impersonal, all-embracing, alive existence, is always here, in every moment. Just like the ugly duckling that was never noticed, which suddenly appears as the princess it had always been.

Regarding habits: If, out of the blue, there is no longer a 'mini-me' which comments and judges your life at every moment, many habits inevitably change too. Old inclinations can return or fade away. Indeed, this can sometimes be quite amazing.

Let me share with you a short anecdote: When I, and thus my mind, read years ago that time doesn't exist, I tried to get used to a timeless state by removing the wristwatch I had worn for many years. I did this, even though I liked watches very much. When, together with the 'mini-me', suddenly time and space disappeared, one of the first things I did was to put on my watch again, because it is very practical in daily life and actually looks rather nice.

∞

What do you tell to people who simply ignore the 'me-thought', say that it will never disappear and that anyway everything is already Being?

When so called 'Oneness concepts' (and this also applies to concepts in general) meet the human mind, generally two things can happen:

1.) The mind occupies itself with these concepts or

2.) The mind leaves them be.

I want to make the second option as appealing as possible.

In the first case, the mind is going to try and explain Oneness by using thought constructs to keep, preserve and institutionalise Oneness. Gradually, the mind will (ab-)use the concept of Oneness for all possible kinds of purposes and try to legitimate everything with it. That's the origin of religions and Non-Duality communities.

In the second case, it can happen that the identification with a personal 'mini-me', and with it the concept of Oneness, both disappear. What remains is, who would have guessed, still Oneness, which is equally also there in the first case.

Both cases are expressions of life. Expressions of Oneness playing the game of life. Both are waves on the ocean of Oneness, which is YOU.

∞

THE SELF IS ALSO THE SELF – FUNNY QUESTION TIME

If consciousness is the only thing that exists, I'm wondering to which 'Self' for example Karl Renz talks to?

Karl Renz can get away with this – he is enlightened. No, seriously; if only the ONE (the Self, Being) exists, then of course Karl Renz, his talks, your question, your confusion about it and my answer are the ONE too. This question-answer-situation appears as a spaceless and timeless event in the ONE. That of course is again another concept, but the concept is the ONE too.

It's like a mirror at the hairdressers which presents endless reflections of your head. Ultimately, everything falls back into the ONE. And the falling back is the ONE too.

∞

Would you rather describe the ONE as 'dead boring' or as 'universal intelligence'?

'Universal' in the sense of 'all-encompassing' sounds quite good. But intelligent? The only thing the ONE needs to be able to do, is to BE. That's easy. Unbelievably easy. You don't have to be intelligent for that. You can't go wrong.

But actually 'universal stupidity' doesn't sound convincing either. Anyhow, the ONE is terribly boring. Nothing happens at all. There is only stupid Oneness, Love, Happiness, Peace and Freedom. Dead boring! Nothing going on. I think I'm going to look for a different ONE.

Joking apart, there is no definition and no blueprint of Oneness. What could be the difference between 'emptiness', 'fullness', 'universal intelligence' or 'nothing going on'? I don't see one. These are just words. You could also say: The ONE is 'fries and ketchup'. It's the same. All there is, is the ONE. (Am I repeating myself?)

∞

I'M ALSO A QUACK DOCTOR

What is the difference between the modern 'Neo-Advaita' and the traditional Advaita Vedanta? Western Neo-Advaita seems to me as if a surgeon operated without education or practical experience.

Because the human mind wants to analyse, classify and then authorise all appearances, it inevitably creates a science out of everything. When the mind occupies itself with Oneness, it approaches it in the same way. By using this method of analysis, the mind splits the One into two or more pieces. It builds a complicated construct of ideas and calls it, for example, 'religious science', 'philosophy' or 'the teachings of Advaita-Vedanta'.

The term 'Neo-Advaita' is a rather unfortunate choice because actually a 'new non-duality' doesn't make any sense at all. 'My' non-dualism doesn't care about the form of traditional Indian Advaita Vedanta. I only borrowed the Sanskrit word 'Advaita' for want of something better.

So forget about Advaita and Neo-Advaita. These terms are an unnecessary burden. It's not a matter of words but of the direct unfiltered communication of something that can't be taught. Here in Europe and not in India. In English and not in Marathi or Tamil language. The non-dual fist smack in the face. For as long as it takes until the mind gives up.

And now to your interesting analogy. I would express it in this way: Where there is no patient, there is no need for a surgeon. The surgeon can't operate a completely healthy human being into more health, no matter how brilliant he is. So the operation is cancelled because it is identified, by 'nobody', as unnecessary (and this 'nobody' doesn't even have a PhD, imagine that).

LET GO OF THE LETTING GO

It is said that one has to get rid of everything in order to get completely liberated. What exactly does this mean?

It's the conditioned idea of human beings in this dual world of time and space that everything must always have a cause. Before complete liberation can occur, something has to happen first, according to the spiritual human mind. For example, something has to be gotten rid of – fear, material things or a particular type of thoughts, etc. Or else a 'gate to enlightenment' must be passed through or a 'jump into freedom' must be made. The list is endless.

But there isn't anybody who could, or has to, get rid of something. Oneness can't let go of Oneness. Nor can Oneness pass through Oneness. Oneness was, is and always will be Oneness. No riches need be disposed of, unless of course you prefer to live under a bridge. Wealth itself IS Oneness. You also don't need to get rid of any thoughts of 'unworthiness'. Those thoughts are Oneness as well.

Liberation doesn't happen BECAUSE of giving something up but rather, if you like, IN SPITE of giving something up. To give up is neither necessary nor obstructive. Oneness was there before the giving up and Oneness will be there afterwards. Just as the waves on the ocean are always there and they are always the ocean. Liberation is exactly NOW.

∞

FROM GURUS AND OTHER PROJECTION SURFACES

My Indian guru says: 'In general, Europeans and Americans are greedy. They are always hunting for prey. He who is not first directly taught the VE-DA (KNOWLEDGE), does not understand Advaita Vedanta.' This guru of ancient Vedic tradition reacts in a very irritated fashion when someone says: 'There is nobody here.' What do you have to say about this?

I can empathise with your guru very well. He was brought up, maybe even drilled, in this old tradition for many years. Suddenly, the ignorant Westerners, the greedy imperialists who once occupied India, come and dilute his precious tradition by misusing 'holy' Sanskrit words.

The main problem seems to be that there are no suitable alternative terms for this kind of 'transmission of Truth' in the western world. If you're in a bookstore or surfing the internet you will find Tony Parsons under the topic or the search term of 'Satsang' or 'Neo-Advaita.' That's the only reason why I use these terms.

As for the concept 'there is nobody': It is exactly this statement of western 'hardcore non-dualists' that resonated very much in my body and gave me the strongest confidence. I never warmed up to the 'holy books' like the Bible, the Bhagavad Gita or the Upanishads. For me the key messages were far too diluted in these traditional books. They used too many words and descriptions. I preferred to get the 'fist of Truth' straight in my face and didn't want to fill my mind with thousands of Indian verses. Yes, perhaps that's the way we Westerners are. Everyone has been conditioned in a different way.

Of course, the core of these writings is nowadays completely clear to me, but only because my mind is no longer getting in the way. For me the detour via holy books and meditation was obviously unnecessary. Clarity appeared together with the awakening. The focus is always on the core of truth, like the finger of the master permanently fixed upon the moon, even if his students continue to study his hand.

∞

But why are we distracted from our freedom with unnecessary entertainment by Madhukar and others? How can we learn to drive a car with a driving instructor who doesn't recognise that the car is driving itself?

Well with the same logic you could argue that you are distracted from your freedom by all my unnecessary words. No, you don't have to learn anything in order to be what you already are. Learning is good for the mind, but the mind doesn't belong to this place.

It seems to be the nature of this psycho-somatic machine called 'human being' to do something in order to maintain the body's tone. If there is no identification with a personal 'mini-me' any more, he normally does what he likes most, is used to doing or has a talent for. In Madhukar's case he gives Satsang with a lot of entertainment. Madhukar, whom I don't know personally, is conditioned in a completely different way to myself. For this reason his Satsang is completely different to mine. The Essence of course is the same – we both understand that nothing has to be done for you to become what you already are. With our different Satsang styles we create the space of possibility where seekers can accept the proposition that a search is completely unnecessary and where the identification can suddenly drop away. If you accept somebody as your guru – the one to lead you out of the darkness and into the light – it doesn't matter what he says or does.

Why do we do what we do? Well, it simply happens. Why I'm answering questions here although I see only Oneness in you is the divine game of life.

In short: If you don't like yoga, meditation, incense sticks and Indian trips you will probably read my book or meet me for a coffee and you won't go to Madhukar's Satsang. And if you prefer to do something completely different, like watching a film, then just do that. That's the ONE too. There is nothing else.

∞

Does Andrew Cohen communicate the Truth too? In our opinion he goes around in circles, but stays close to the core. Do you see any similarities with your personal style of teaching?

Truth cannot be taught. Everything that happens occurs in a timeless and spaceless Oneness, including Andrew Cohen and his teachings. They are not separate from you or from me. Whatever he tells you, what you should do or not do to reach liberation, is exactly THAT which appears and is therefore perfect. It is THAT. If his words please you and if you trust him, this will be your path, or rather it will be the path of the psychosomatic apparatus you believe to be 'you'. Or else you will look for another teacher, or you may throw in the towel, because you've had enough of all this.

That's the film of life, which appears IN YOU, in Oneness. It doesn't matter what Andrew Cohen says. He cannot make more or less out of you than that which you already are. Oneness. With the apparent liberation of Andrew Cohen you have been liberated as well. Whether you go to Andrew

Cohen, come to me or go to the theatre doesn't really matter. What you are looking for is HERE, in every moment.

∞

My Indian guru says: 'You are Love.' Okay, I say, but then I am also envy and hate! He didn't like this at all. What do you, as an approved Satsang teacher, have to say about this?

My answer as an 'approved Satsang teacher' comes directly from common sense, which has quite a helpful function in daily life:

If your guru teaches in a dualistic way (your question points to that) and if his concept says that, what you really are, the 'True Self', is Love, then envy and hate, two of the mortal sins, represent the polar opposite. They represent something, which, according to his concept, you have to renounce. With his concept your guru wants to help you to become a more loving, 'better' person. Religions ask the same from their followers. It is a kind of spiritual re-education which your guru is offering you.

If you counter his well-intended offer with your non-dual arguments, you won't get anywhere. It is as if a Catholic tried to dissuade the Pope from Catholicism with mere mind games. If, according to the axiom of non-duality, everything is One, of course you are also envy and hate. You are also spaghetti. So what? That is not the point. Your guru offers you a gift with his statement and you reject it by questioning him with non-dual thought concepts. No wonder he doesn't like this, because he sees that you are knocking on the wrong door. That is the game of life and you have just violated the game rules of your guru. Get over it.

You question my lovely guru (a Brahman)! He is not a chocolate seller. He would never say 'all is ONE... or that IS = SHOULD BE. He says: you are THAT and your reality as a human being is THAT.

Well, every teacher, master or guru, whether Brahman, Buddhist, Christian or Muslim, is in a certain way a chocolate seller (I love this metaphor). I'm one too. By using words we are trying to sell you the mystery that the search for enlightenment (chocolate!) is unnecessary. That you already have your fridge full of chocolate! In fact we are bad salesmen because we don't sell you anything at all. We see that you already have everything and we tell you this. That's all! One does it in a dualistic way, the other in a non-dualistic way. Everyone does it the way he has learned it and the way he can do it best. It doesn't matter with which hand the master points to the moon and what his hand looks like: big or small, fat or thin, smooth or hairy, clean or dirty. The hand is not important, only the moon matters.

∞

Could you please interpret Papaji's metaphor of 'the rope that is seen to have been a snake the whole time'?

To make sure that everyone knows what we're talking about I shall explain the metaphor:

'You are scared to cross the road, on the other side of which lies freedom, because you see a snake there coiled up in the middle of the road, waiting for you. Every day you come back, you see the snake and you are afraid to go on. One day somebody comes from the other side and says: 'It's only a rope. There is no snake, just a rope.' This authority tells the truth and you recognise it. What is happening here? What have you done with the snake? Where did it go? 'I am bound' is just this snake. The snake never existed. You have to overcome the obstacles 'fear' and 'doubt'. See the rope for what it is.'

Papaji is talking about faith. Satsang only works if there is faith in the one who says that the snake (world of duality) is illusionary. That it's only a rope (Oneness). But actually nothing happens at all. The supposed snake was a rope before and is still a rope afterwards. The 'mini-me', however, will always think that the rope is a snake. It can't help it. In the moment of the disappearance (death) of the 'mini-me', the snake is seen as a rope, but not by the 'mini-me'. It's absolute seeing. The road (separation), the master, the snake, the rope and the disciple all dissolve in this seeing and become ONE.

No one can bring about faith in another. No teacher, master or guru. He can tell you again and again that you have to overcome fear and doubts. Faith simply appears, just like this book just appears for you. (Yes, exactly NOW, JUST for you!) It is a kind of deep resonance and a remembering of the past, a knowing that what is said here must be true.

I keep saying it again and again: there are no obstacles! The story of the rope is only a metaphor for the spiritual mind. Just forget it. The road has never existed.

In my opinion the following picture describes accurately the desperate situation of a spiritual seeker. By chance there is also a rope involved:

A spiritual seeker believes he is hanging on a rope above a deadly abyss. He holds the rope tightly with his two hands and is convinced that he will fall to his death if he lets go of the rope. Because he is so focused on the abyss and the rope above him, he overlooks the fact that he is actually standing with his feet firmly on the ground. I stand next to him and use my words to explain to him this fact, knowing that he is safe. But unfortunately I can't release his fingers from the rope. I can use only my words to create faith. When faith appears, the rope is released. And nothing changes because everything was already perfect in the first place.

∞

Theoretically the words of H.W.L. Poonja: 'From the first not a thing is. From the outset your nature is free' seem to be plausible to us. However, can you help us understand how this relates to our daily life?

In other words Poonja says: 'There is nothing to be done in order to be free. It is your True Nature to be free.'

You cannot become something that you are already inherently. Therefore Poonja advises you to be silent. With 'silent' he doesn't mean that you are not allowed to speak or that you have to start meditating. No, he says that you can't do anything wrong because you are already free. There is nothing that hampers you from being free. That is the ABSOLUTE silence which is here in every moment, whatever you do. It can't be easier, can it? This silence is your True Nature. Being. Oneness. Pure existence which is closer to you than anything else you can imagine, because you ARE already this.

∞

In our opinion Gandhi's message 'be the change you want to see in the world' applies exactly to you as a pointer and teacher! How would YOU express this message, since actually no 'change' is necessary?

With his words Gandhi refers to the role model of a teacher which, governed by the laws of cause and effect of this dual (illusory) world, is best suited to bring about a change of habits in daily life, because it creates faith. Quite in line with the motto: 'You reap what you sow'. In this sense my function here is as that of a teacher who creates faith with his words.

However, my non-dual 'message' (in contrast to Gandhi's dual message) inevitably generates paradoxical situations as soon as words come into play. On the one hand I tell you with many words that you should have faith, and on the other hand I say that, in order to reach freedom, no change is needed because liberation is already here NOW. In my eyes you are already liberated and ONE with me and everything. The liberation of the whole world simultaneously occurred with the liberation of the apparent individual.

But why this message at all? Well, this 'message' is in fact not needed since you, Gandhi and myself are ONE timeless and spaceless occurrence that apparently happens in Oneness. Without any cause and any meaning. In reality it hasn't actually happened, because there is only Oneness. Gandhi appears IN YOU, so to speak. You are Gandhi. Therefore you can relax, sit back and forget about all the teachers and guides who want to convey any old truth to you regarding awakening and liberation. Liberation happened simultaneously with the apparent separation from Oneness.

∞

HELLO, BEING IS SPEAKING

What actually is it which communicates through you? Does anything happen at all when we attend your Satsang? 'Newcomers' always use their minds, because they want to understand. Do they have to first let go of what they have read in order to find IT? It seems to be insufficient if you tell us that we aren't blind. Do we have to be aware of the fact that SEEING always IS?

If you go to a teacher you consciously or unconsciously assimilate the experience through your mind and your senses. If the 'chemistry' is good between you and your teacher, you believe him. That's called faith. It can't be enforced.

People who visit me are often quite amazed what a normal guy I am. I'm the guy to drink coffee, have a beer or go to the cinema with. They don't see an unapproachable Indian guru sitting in front of them, but somebody who looks and speaks like them. That calms them down a lot and allows them to finish the search.

You don't have to be aware of the fact that SEEING is always here. If your mind has understood my metaphor of the glasses in this way, then unfortunately this picture is wrong for you. It's quite tricky with these pictures and allegories! No, you don't have to do ANYTHING. Just live the way life lives you. Every moment is perfect. The moments of seeking and despair too. Relax and just do something you would do anyway, without being forced to and don't think about why you are doing it. That's all.

∞

GOOD TIMES, BAD TIMES

Are relationships with one, or even better two, realised partners easier than 'normal' relationships? Because, if Oneness accepts everything as it is, the 'knowing' partner should always comply.

Let me quickly ask my wife if she is enlightened. No, honestly, Oneness accepts everything, people don't. Oneness cannot have relationships, people can. You generally could say that with the disappearance of a personal identification there is more honesty and authenticity. Of course this can have a varied impact on a relationship, as you can imagine: if you withdraw into a cave your wife will probably leave you.

Suppose you like spaghetti and detest cauliflower. You will probably remain with these preferences your whole life, if the outer circumstances allow. Therefore, you will generally prefer to be close with the people you feel attracted to (where the 'chemistry' is right) and will have a relationship with them, regardless of whether you are 'realised' or not.

∞

And how can we use your metaphor of the ocean with that question? What is the ocean, what are the waves?

The ocean is Oneness, the waves are the forms of the dual world, which includes also people consisting of thoughts and bodies (thought forms). One single wave has no influence on how it is constructed and how it will behave. Whether it prefers spaghetti or cauliflower or to which other wave it feels attracted. But if the wave identifies with a person (the 'mini-me') and imagines itself to be separated from the other waves and from the ocean, then it doesn't accept this fact. It has the feeling that it is the actor with free will. Metaphorically speaking, it will interact with other waves according to the physical laws (conditioning), connect with them (have a relationship), split again (separation of a relationship), disappear (death) or appear (birth). This all happens in the ocean. It IS the ocean. It is what you, the wave, really is. Being.

∞

AM I ENLIGHTENED NOW, OR WHAT?

When I listen to teachers talking about truth and awakening, I can't help thinking that I've always been in that state. But since a couple of years I feel as if there is a filter between 'me' and 'reality'. Together with that filter an intense tiredness has appeared; a tension and sometimes a depression, along with a strong flow of thinking. Last year I began to experience a deep peace in which all struggle ceases. But I'm still not 'satisfied' with it. I keep on falling into suffering cycles and I have the 'knowledge', if I may say so, that even in deepest peace I am not at the 'maximum potential' of Being.

What you are describing to me seems to be different states of your body-mind-complex which confuse you, because you interpret and would like to understand them. When awakening occurs (the realisation that you are pure Being and not the 'mini-me') and together with this awakening this deep peace appears, the 'mini-me' wants to conserve this agreeable state immediately. It starts to identify with the state of deep peace. But if some change happens, for example if emotions like sadness or anger appear, the 'mini-me' is very disappointed because these emotions don't fit its idealised picture of an enlightened person.

Complete liberation means that the 'mini-me' has given up trying to grab hold of the desirable awakened state and push away other undesirable states. The 'mini-me' doesn't want to pilot the divine vehicle of life any more. It accepts the fact that no pilot is needed and that no pilot was ever needed. In this absolute freedom EVERYTHING is allowed to happen. It happens IN what you are. Just allow it to happen and don't worry about it. Nothing has to be done or changed in order for liberation.

∞

Please tell us blind ones something amazing so that at least one (!) of our eyes finally opens.

There is nothing 'more' to see than that which is already here and now, whether with one eye or two. I don't see any more than you. You see, if you like, 'apparently' more than I. Or better said: you think you see more. You interpret more from that which just IS.

But even this interpretation is the invitation of Oneness to accept liberation as what it is; the most normal thing you can imagine. Therefore, nothing dazzling is needed. Isn't it already stunning that NOTHING separates you from freedom? I can neither give you something nor take something away from you, because it is not necessary. Relax and don't wait for a special incident. The state of waiting IS the incident! You have your glasses on and your eyes open. Celebrate this fact every moment. The banal, unglamorous and unspiritual paper pages of this book that you are looking at right now ARE IT.

∞

But, do you mean that I just can go home, bake a cake and read the newspaper? Is it exactly that?

Yes exactly. But I want to have a piece of cake too!

∞

A reader writes:

*'If you seriously search for something, whatever it is,
you will find it in Oliver's answers.
Read them more than once and trust him.
Please! It is worth it!'*

'I can write words. Whether they lead to faith or not is Grace.'

Oliver

∞

'I AM. I EXIST. That is all.
I am BEFORE birth and death, BEFORE all concepts.
Before the world was, I AM.'

∞

THE AUTHOR

Oliver Bosshard was born in Zurich, Switzerland in 1970. Today he lives in Winterthur, Switzerland. This book is his gift to the spiritual seeker who is sick of the eternal search.

Satsang with Oliver Bosshard is pure non-dualism without compromises and stands beyond religions, philosophies and beliefs.

Oliver is not a guru. He is a silent companion who, with a portion of humour, accompanies all concepts of the searching person ad absurdum, till Nothing remains. This 'Nothing' is THAT which has always been longed for. It's the end of a journey which never began.

∞

THE ESSENCE

∞

'I don't teach anything because nothing can be added to
what is already complete.'

∞

'Liberation is always closer than you think.'

∞

'Calm down and forget about enlightenment.
It's only a concept, one among millions of concepts.
An empty construct of thoughts which emerges out of what you ARE.
Oneness.'

∞

'There is no enlightened person.
If enlightenment happens, it happens for 'nobody'.
Enlightenment can be equated with the disappearance of the person
who wants to be enlightened.'

∞

'The merciless Being doesn't know Grace because it IS Grace itself.'

∞

'Grace is always present.
Grace is the only thing there is.
Grace can't be given to somebody and you can't prepare for it.
Grace is the invitation, the gift from Being to itself to accept,
that all there is, is THIS.
The ONE, the Essence of you.'

∞

'Nobody, no person, no teacher, master or guru
can make awakening happen. Neither can I,
because there is nobody who can choose if, when,
and to whom 'it' happens.
And that's fine, because actually nothing has to happen at all.
Liberation already occurred simultaneously with the apparent separation
from Oneness.'

∞

'The glasses of Truth you believed to have lost
and which you are now desperately looking for are still on your nose.
Accept the gift. It's Grace. Just look through them
as you always have done. And enjoy clear-sightedness.'

∞

'If you try to keep and conserve Truth it's no Truth any more'

∞

'You don't have to become a gentle, pure, religious or spiritual human being in order to be worthy of liberation.
Liberation is already here NOW, always, in every moment.'

∞

'If you think you need to do something,
just carry a feeling with you of how it would be,
if you had already found what you are looking for.'

∞

'There are no obstacles on the path to liberation.
The only apparent obstacle is the conviction that there is an obstacle.
And even that conviction is in fact no obstacle, because it is what appears in this moment and therefore is completely perfect.'

∞

'The timeless moment is always perfect.
Even if, let's say, you are eating and watching TV at the same time.
It's Oneness appearing as a person who is eating and watching TV.
Everything that happens is THAT. It appears in you; in pure awareness.

It's not you, but it's the manifestation which has been conditioned
for aeons. A present manifestation of the Divine.'

∞

'All there is, is IT.'

∞

'The conviction that there is an obstacle on the way to enlightenment
is only one (!) among countless empty thoughts which arise from Being
and disappear again, like waves on the ocean.
It's the destiny of the waves to arise and disappear.

∞

'You don't need to be awakened because you are not asleep.'

∞

'Free will is an illusion of mind.'

∞

'There is nobody who could choose to do anything,
let alone to awaken. There also isn't anybody who could teach awakening.
There is neither a disciple nor a master. There is only THAT. Being.

It is the learning, the teaching and the learnt at the same time.
It emerges out of what you are. It is what you are.'

∞

'Forget about my concept of not having a free will,
the concept of the endless happiness and freedom
that you've been searching for and just let life live you.'

∞

'Being doesn't care about the film of life which runs anyway
just as it must. The screenplay is written, the film is shot
and all characters are played by you.
You are the screen on which the film is projected,
you are the light and you are the audience.
You even are the popcorn and the M&Ms.'

∞

'You are the feather in the wind. And you are the wind.'

∞

'Everything that happens to you as an apparent body-mind-complex
is perfect.'

'There is no 'what would have happened, if…'
Life never misses you. That's the game.
The game has no impact on your Essence.
The Essence of you is Oneness.'

∞

'There is nothing to be recognised because for absolute awareness
there is neither somebody who recognises (subject)
nor something that can be recognised (object).
There isn't anybody who could have the awareness of enlightenment.
One could only say that when enlightenment happens,
the impersonal knowing appears that all that happens in every moment
is the ONE, the perfect One.'

∞

'I am like the seer among the blind who sees that nobody is blind.'

∞

'I don't teach. Through my words Oneness shows Oneness the absurdity
of the game of separation.'

∞

'My words are like the mantra of the master who says
that there is neither a master nor a need for one.'

'You want to be free? Then don't look at the completely irrelevant finger of
the master when he shows you the moon.
Stop trying to find a link between the finger (dualism)
and the moon (non-dualism) using thought concepts.
It's neither possible nor necessary. Have faith and look at the moon.
Clarity will arise automatically.'

∞

'There is only the ONE without a second.'

∞

'Oneness can't be reached and nothing has to be done to reveal Oneness.
It can't be comprehended by the mind and it can't be described
with words. Words can only be a pointer to the Truth.'

∞

'The final realisation doesn't happen BECAUSE of the words of this book,
but, if you like, IN SPITE of them.'

∞

'The last step of the spiritual journey, the 'jump into enlightenment',
can't and doesn't have to occur, because there is neither a journey
nor enlightenment.'

'Spiritual search and enlightenment are One.
All apparent problems point back to the one (!) thought of separation
which began in early childhood.
They come from the conviction of being a human body,
a separated thing with a free will,
which has to survive and defend itself in the world.'

∞

'Everything appears in you, nothing is separated from you.
The world appears in you, not the other way around.'

∞

'It doesn't matter what your character is or what appears in your life,
because it has nothing to do with you as Essence.
It appears IN you, in pure awareness.'

∞

'In the end concepts won't liberate you.
Books filled with concepts only feed the mind.'

∞

'The only concept which leads to what can't be reached by concepts
is the acceptance that all concepts are unnecessary.'

'It doesn't matter with which finger the master points to the moon
or what this finger looks like. If it is big or small, thick or thin,
smooth or hairy, clean or dirty. The finger is irrelevant.
Only the moon matters.'

∞

'Liberation doesn't occur because you let go of something but, if you will,
EVEN THOUGH you let go of something.'

∞

'The human mind is the perfect knife. Its only purpose is to divide.
Everything has to be divided and built into a system.
That's perfect because without mind it would be impossible
to handle our daily life.'

∞

'If the razor-sharp mind tries to understand Oneness,
it inevitably fails. A knife is used to cut, not to join together.'

∞

'The glue which joins duality together with Oneness
is the not-wanting-to-understand.'

'Life, the divine game, is like a chess board
with an infinite number of squares, and it can never be won
with the tactics of the human mind.'

∞

'Complete silence doesn't result from the absence of thoughts,
but rather from the absence of the person
who identifies with these thoughts.'

∞

'I am even though I think.'

∞

www.ingramcontent.com/pod-product-compliance
Lightning Source LLC
Chambersburg PA
CBHW021021090426
42738CB00007B/853